Dorie Miller:

Greatness Under Fire

By Dante R. Brizill

Copyright 2018 by Dante R. Brizill

Publisher: Kindle Direct Publisher

Cover Art and design: Robert Gussio

Editor: Donna Murphy

Ordering Information

This book may be purchased in large quantities for educational use. For more information, email dbrizill@icloud.com.

Request Dante

To request Dante R. Brizill for a keynote address, speaking engagement, workshop, or seminar, email dbrizill@icloud.com

Advance Praise

"This is a compelling account of the life of Dorie Miller, an African-American messman in the U.S. Navy. The author outlines Dorie Miller's life in the true fashion of a teacher, from Mr. Miller's humble beginnings in Texas, to his heroic acts at Pearl Harbor. Through Brizill's detailed, factual storytelling, the reader is intrigued and led to learn even more about the history of Mr. Miller and Pearl Harbor. The author even challenges the reader to find personal ways to be a hero. This book would serve as a great supplement to African-American History curricula and would be a benefit to American History classes.

-Dr. Eugina Smith Feaman, Middle School Principal

"Every American should know about Dorie Miller. Brizill does a great job of both setting the historical context and telling the story of Miller's heroism at Pearl Harbor. I couldn't agree more with Brizill's last line-"Let's keep this story alive!"

-Steve Sheinkin, author of The Port Chicago 50

Table of Contents

Author's Note

I am excited to finally share the story of Dorie Miller after years of research. The story of Pearl Harbor is well known and has been recounted countless times, but Dorie's story was not always included. Ever since I came across his name years ago, I wanted to know more, and the more that I found out, the more that I wanted to tell his story. This book is not intended to be the definitive work on Dorie Miller or an academic research project. There have been other iterations of this extraordinary young man's story in print, which may fit those descriptions, but this book is intended to introduce young Americans to a genuine American hero. Hopefully this book will give a little more context to the man that was played briefly but masterfully by Cuba Gooding Jr. in Pearl Harbor. History does not have to be boring. The more we uncover stories like Dorie's, the more we can make history come alive.

I would like to take this opportunity to thank God, my lovely wife for her unending support, family, friends, students and colleagues who have encouraged me over the years to write and share my knowledge of history beyond the classroom. Special thanks to the following individuals for your help and support in helping me to make this story become a reality: Dr Nancy Fox for your words of wisdom, my editor Donna Murphy for your time and effort with the manuscript, Bob Gussio for the outstanding cover design, Elkton High Media Specialist Karen Dietz for your kindness and assistance, Pamela Avery and Virginia Rector there aren't enough words to describe your influence, and last but not least award winning author Steve Sheinkin who mentored me through this process from afar . Being an educator myself, I would be remiss not to give a shout out to the teachers and professors who collectively inspired me to get into the mother of all professions, who taught me to revise, edit and tell a good story.

Dante R. Brizill

October 2018

Dedication

This book is dedicated to my two grandfathers for their honorable service to this country. Livingston Brizill Sr. (1924-1999) served in a segregated United States Marine Corps in World War II and David Dorn, Sr. (1932-2000) who served in the Korean War.

Livingston Brizill Sr. was one of the first black enlistees in the Marines from Philadelphia in World War II. David

Dorn, Sr. served in the Korean War and for a period of time was listed as missing in action for months in enemy territory. Both safely returned to their families.

Pop-pops,

Thank you for being my first heroes. Thank you for the memories and the impression you left upon me in my youth. Even now I look back occasionally and smile at a word of wisdom you imparted to me, and quality time well spent. You are truly missed. I hope that I have made you proud. -Dante

Introduction

What comes to your mind when you hear the word hero? Do you think of a firefighter running into a burning building to rescue a child or a lifeguard at the beach running toward a drowning swimmer? Do you think of someone who rises above their fear and does something extraordinary? Tragedies often produces heroes, and December 7th, 1941 was no different. It was a horrible day in American history. Japan launched a surprise attack on the United States naval base at **Pearl Harbor** in Hawaii. Over 2,000 American sailors and soldiers lost their lives on that tragic day, and another 1,000 were injured. Many of them never had a chance to fight back, but one of the many who was able to respond was Doris "Dorie" Miller. This is his story, the story of a young man who dreamed big dreams, who rose from humble roots and who went above and beyond the call of duty on a day that President Franklin Delano Roosevelt called "A date that will live in infamy".

Texas Roots

Doris Miller was born on October 12, 1919 in Waco, Texas the third of four sons. Those who knew him called him "Dorie". He was originally named Doris. The midwife who assisted his mother in delivery thought that he would be a girl. Somehow over time he became known as "Dorie" perhaps due to the fact of a typo. His parents were **sharecroppers**. This is the life that many African-Americans were subject to in the American South in the early 20th century. Dorie was always big for his age eventually reaching 6'3 200 pounds. Young Dorie assisted his family around the 28-acre farm and could not begin the school year until the cotton crop was harvested. Dorie was not a great student, but due to his size and strength, he was a good athlete. He was a standout baseball pitcher and he played the position of fullback on the football team for Waco's A.J. Moore High School. Dorie's athleticism earned him the nickname "Power". Dorie did not return to school after the 8th grade. Instead he did what he could to try to support his family. He unsuccessfully tried to join the Civilian Conservation Corps. This was a program created during the Great Depression to put young men to work who needed jobs conserving our natural resources and forestry.

He tried to join the army, but his father would not agree to sign the consent papers. Like most small-town boys his age, young Dorie dreamed of seeing the world, and looked toward joining the military. During this time period, it was not uncommon for young men to join the military to escape the poverty of the Great Depression and to help to support their struggling families back home. Can you imagine young Dorie after a hard day of work on the farm in the unforgiving Texas heat, dreaming of a better life for himself and his parents, or imagining faraway places? In September of 1939, a month before his twentieth birthday he enlisted in the U.S. Navy.

During the 1940's the U.S. Navy was not the friendliest place for a young African-American man looking for opportunity. The armed forces practiced **segregation** during World War II. African-American service-men lived and fought in units separate from white soldiers, sailors and marines during the war and often had to do jobs that required manual labor. Few of these units were sent to combat zones.

Dorie was familiar with segregation growing up. It was practiced in his home state of Texas as it was elsewhere in the American South. The Navy was no different, and this was the environment that Dorie was entering.

African-American men in the Navy during that time were only allowed to be mess attendants. A mess attendant's job was to prepare and serve food and clear dirty tables. They were not trained to operate the weaponry on the ships or perform any other duties. They even had to wear different uniforms. Although African-Americans demanded better treatment and more opportunities in the military throughout World War II, change would come slowly. Can you imagine the disappointment Dorie must have felt when he found out that he could only prepare and serve meals and clean tables? Despite this low ranked job, Dorie performed his duties with excellence, and was eventually promoted to the post of

Ship's Cook, Third Class. Dorie trained at the Naval training station in Norfolk, Virginia. In 1940, he was transferred to the USS West Virginia. While he served on that ship, he was temporarily assigned to another battleship the USS Nevada to the Secondary Battery Gunnery School. As an African-American in the segregated military, Dorie was limited to being a messman. As a result, he was only trained to pass ammunition to the sailors instructed on how to fire the gun. After his training was complete, he went back to the USS West Virginia. Probably due to Dorie's size, strength, and athletic skill, he became the ship's heavyweight boxing champion! This would come in handy for him, when his country needed him most. Soon the West

Virginia was ordered to Pearl Harbor as

tensions between the United States and

Japan increased.

The African-American experience in World War II

On December 8th, 1941 one day after the surprise Japanese attack on Pearl Harbor, **President Franklin D. Roosevelt** went before a joint session of Congress and   asked for a Declaration of War. As Americans gathered around their radio sets, they knew that they would be called upon to sacrifice and support the war effort in the coming months and years ahead. African-Americans served with distinction in every war since the American revolution.

Of the 16 million Americans who served in World War II, approximately one million of them were African-American men and women. The armed forces that they entered would discriminate against them and subject them to inferior roles and jobs because of the color of their skin. It was a commonly held belief by many in the military leadership that African-Americans were not capable enough to perform duties that required specialized training and skill. They also believed that the military should not be used as a place to promote racial equality. These assumptions were not challenged by

Congress and the President forcefully, although Roosevelt did push the armed services to admit more African-Americans. It was up to black newspapers and Civil Rights organizations to press the issue of equality and openness in the military. Many black servicemen had to settle for driving trucks, loading and unloading ships, and working in kitchens and mess halls rather than going into combat.

There were some notable exceptions, like the famed **Tuskegee Airmen** also known as the "Red Tails" because of the red colored paint on the tails of their planes. This decorated unit of African-American pilots shot down 111 enemy aircraft, destroyed 150 on the ground and sunk a German ship. Like Dorie, they proved that they could rise above racist labels and perform at a high level when given the opportunity.

Another standout unit was the 761st Tank Battalion also known as "**Patton's Panthers**". This highly decorated unit received 7 Silver Stars, 56 Bronze stars, and 246 Purple Hearts. It is difficult to understand the story of Dorie Miller without first understanding the African-American experience in America during World War II.

By the time America entered World War II in 1941 the United States was a deeply segregated country. The Supreme Court decision in 1896 in the infamous **Plessy vs. Ferguson** case established the doctrine of "separate but equal". In the South it was by law while in the North it was by custom. Blacks and whites lived in separate neighborhoods and went to separate schools. The facilities were separate and unequal. The armed forces were no different. There were only 5,000 African-Americans in the Navy at the start of the war America entered in 1941. The Marines and Army Air Corp refused to even admit blacks until later in the war. Ever since the Civil War black soldiers fought in separate units led by white officers. This tradition was continued throughout World War II. At age 20, Dorie Miller was entering a segregated navy that would only admit African-Americans as cooks.

These segregationist policies were unacceptable to many African-Americans as the United States prepared for war. The humiliating experience and the treatment of black soldiers in World War I were resented by many African-American veterans, political leaders and newspaper editors. In that war 380,000 African-Americans enlisted to fight, but very few saw combat due to the racist attitudes of the era. The few units that did see combat were attached to French units and distinguished themselves well in battle. Black veterans from that war were denied benefits and disability payments. At least 13 of them were lynched after returning home. It was well known by black veterans that being seen in uniform could be extremely dangerous. These leaders were determined that in the next war they would demand better treatment and equality for the black soldier.

President Roosevelt knew that he had to keep the peace at home in order to successfully fight our enemies overseas. Racial tensions escalated as African-Americans in large numbers left the fields and moved to where the factory jobs were. Under pressure, the President signed an executive order banning job discrimination in the war industries after labor leader **A. Phillip Randolph** threatened a march on Washington. His executive order also established the **Fair Employment Practices Committee** to investigate cases of discrimination. It was a small start, but a step in the right direction. Shortly after the United States entered the war, a widely read black newspaper called *The Pittsburgh Courier* came up with the "**Double V**" campaign in response to a letter it received from an African-American cafeteria worker in Kansas. "Should I sacrifice to live half American?" the

26 year old writer of the letter asked. The "Double V" represented the two battles that African-Americans had to fight: Racism at home and our enemies abroad. This campaign became popular with readers and increased the circulation of the paper. The newspaper ran a weekly feature whose purpose was to increase knowledge of African-Americans who were fighting for their country and to fight for equal treatment under the law when they returned home.

Dories Miller's Ship: The USS West Virginia

Prior to World War II battleships were the ultimate rulers of the oceans. These gigantic sea monsters could inflict significant battle damage on an opponent's surface fleet when engaged in combat. All of the great military powers of the world had a large number of battleships serving in their navies. They were known as *dreadnoughts.* These big ships could hurl shells as large as one thousand pounds, miles into enemy territory on sea, and on land. On December 1, 1923, the USS West Virginia was commissioned. Nicknamed the *Wee-Vee*, this was the ship on which Dorie served. Before an early 1920's conference in Washington that limited the size of naval ships, this was the last American Battleship to be launched. Because the West Virginia was one of the last ships to be built before the conference, it was fitted with the latest naval technology and architecture of that time. During the years between 1923 and the beginning of World War II, the ship underwent upgrades and repairs. As international tensions flared, leading up to the start of World War II, the West Virginia was moved to the naval base in Hawaii where it went through combat training through the year of 1941.

December 7th, 1941 was an ordinary Sunday for most Americans. It was a day when many Americans went to their houses of worship and enjoyed Sunday dinner with their families. World War II, the most violent and destructive conflict in World History had been raging for over two years in Europe, but it had not touched American shores. Many Americans only knew about the war from dramatic radio broadcasts out of London, as well as newspapers, and newsreel footage in their movie theatres. This was how Americans received their news before the invention of the television. Most Americans had never even heard of Pearl Harbor, where our massive naval base in Hawaii headquartered our

Pacific fleet. It was a dream assignment for a young sailor with tropical beaches and beautiful weather.

The United States and Japan did not see eye to eye in the months and weeks leading up to their surprise attack on December 7th. Japan had become an aggressive empire with plans to gobble up territory in Asia, as it waged a brutal and destructive war in China in the 1930's. Beginning in the late 1930's the United States started to restrict trade with Japan. In 1940 the United States decided to place an embargo on oil and other supplies to Japan. An embargo is when a government stops trade with another as a form of punishing the other country. This action further inflamed tensions between the two countries. Eventually the Japanese government decided that it was time to act and remove the United States as an obstacle to their aggression. They thought that destroying our Pacific naval fleet stationed at Pearl Harbor would do the trick.

A Hero Is Made

Pearl Harbor is located in Hawaii, a group of islands which became a U.S. territory in 1898. In 1908, Congress approved the construction of a naval base there. Over the years the base was expanded to include marines as well as artillery and infantry units. On the morning of December 7th, 1941 Dorie Miller was collecting laundry. Earlier he had volunteered as a room steward to make extra money. This job involved providing wake-up services, washing laundry and shining shoes for the ship's officers. Suddenly Japanese airplanes appeared in the skies over Pearl

Harbor. Their mission was to destroy the American Pacific fleet. There were dive bombers and torpedo bombers who had trained for this very day. There were over 300 planes with highly skilled Japanese pilots. They had studied pictures of the American ships that would be at Pearl Harbor that day, and had rehearsed their attacks. These planes were loaded with armored piercing bombs and specially modified torpedoes that could navigate the shallow waters of Pearl Harbor. Several warnings and alarms were sounded before the attack, but they were not taken seriously. The sailors and soldiers at Pearl Harbor were taken by surprise. Dorie

Miller's ship the USS West Virginia was one of the targets.

Imagine being a sailor sleeping on your bunk and awakened to the sound of hundreds of airplanes in the skies, and your ship violently shaking from loud explosions. The sound of loud voices shouting commands, and the terror of sailors screaming in pain filled the air. Dorie had been awake since 6:00 am to perform his normal duties which included collecting dirty laundry. He heard the alarm sound ordering the men to their battle stations. The gun to which Dorie was assigned to provide ammunition was damaged by Japanese torpedoes. He went to another part of the ship to receive other

orders. The ships communications officer

noticed Dorie and ordered him to help move

the ship's seriously wounded captain Mervyn

Bennison to safety. After that he was asked

by another officer to help him load one of the

anti-aircraft guns. The officer became

distracted by something else. When he looked

back, he saw Dorie firing one of the guns "as

though he had fired one all his life" according

to one of the witnesses. Dorie fired at the

attacking planes until he was out of

ammunition. Shortly after he was ordered to

abandon ship along with his fellow shipmates.

(Rescue boats attempt to reach survivors from the USS

West Virginia. Source: US Navy)

It has been claimed that Dorie shot

down six planes, but in the chaos of battle that

has not been verified. His exhibit at the

National African American History Museum in Washington D.C. credits him with downing two enemy planes. What we do know is that Dorie helped to save lives. "It wasn't hard," said Miller. "I just pulled the trigger and she worked fine. I had watched the others with these guns. I guess I fired her for about 15 minutes. I think I got one of those Jap planes. They were diving pretty close to us." Along with numerous other battleships the West Virginia took a heavy punishment that morning after being hit by numerous torpedoes and bombs. It leaked fuel for 30 hours and eventually caught fire. Sadly, many sailors were trapped inside the ship as it sank. Some survived for as many as 16 days before they died, unable to be reached by rescuers who could hear tapping coming from below by trapped sailors. In June of the following year when the ship was hauled to dry dock, the bodies of an additional 66 men were found. Of the 1,541 men on the West Virginia, 130 men were killed and 52 were wounded. The West Virginia would eventually be repaired and would participate in later battles of the war.

African-American messman on a Navy cruiser during

World War II in 1942. (Source: National Archives)

Above and Beyond the Call of Duty by David Stone

Martin, 1943)

Illustration of Miller defending the fleet at Pearl Harbor (Charles Alston, Office of War Information and Public Relations)

The damage done at Pearl Harbor was significant. This surprise attack by the Japanese claimed the lives of 2,403 Americans, damaged or sank 18 ships and destroyed over 100 airplanes. President Roosevelt went before Congress the following day and asked for a declaration of war against Japan. He declared December 7th, 1941 a "date that will live in infamy." Soon after on December 11th, Japan's ally, Germany, declared war on the United States. Practically overnight America was transformed into a war time nation.

Many heroes were created that day, and young Dorie was one of them. It was hard to keep secret the heroic actions of Dorie Miller, on that unforgettable Sunday. The Navy did not publicize Dories actions at first. Initial reports did not identify him, but soon his name became known because many people had witnessed his courage. News of Dorie Miller's heroic actions spread quickly throughout the United States in both black and white communities. The **NAACP** wrote to the Secretary of the Navy, **Frank Knox**, urging him to recognize and honor Dorie for his actions. An African-American newspaper *The Pittsburgh Courier* sent a reporter to find out who this hero was. This same newspaper started a letter writing campaign to convince President Roosevelt to award Dorie for his actions. They weren't alone. The Negro Youth Conference launched a campaign in in April of 1942 on Dorie's behalf. In May of the same year the National Negro Conference criticized Secretary Knox for failing to award Dorie the Medal of Honor. Efforts to award him the **Congressional Medal of Honor** were defeated in Congress. One wonders how much young Dorie was aware of all the people who were pulling for him. Secretary of Navy Frank Knox who was not friendly to the idea of an integrated Navy, was just satisfied with Dorie receiving a congratulatory letter. It was not until the following spring that the Navy revealed who this Negro mess attendant who had been so heroic was. At the intervention of

President Franklin D. Roosevelt, in May of

1942, Dorie was awarded the **Navy Cross** by

Admiral Chester W. Nimitz and was

promoted to Mess Attendant First class. This

is what the citation stated:

> For distinguished devotion to duty, extraordinary
> courage and disregard for his own personal safety
> during the attack on the Fleet in Pearl Harbor,
> territory of Hawaii, by Japanese forces on December 7th 1941.
> While at the side of his Captain on the bridge, despite enemy
> strafing and bombing and in the face of a serious fire,
> assisted in moving his Captain, who had been mortally
> wounded, to a place of greater safety, and later manned and
> operated a machine gun directed at enemy Japanese attacking
> aircraft until ordered to leave the bridge.

(Dorie Miller being awarded the Navy Cross by Admiral Nimitz. Official U.S. Navy photograph)

In a 2001 National Geographic documentary on the 60th anniversary of the attack on Pearl Harbor, a couple of the survivors of the attack stated their opinions that Dorie Miller deserved more than just the Navy Cross.

As was common with war heroes, Dorie was sent on a nationwide tour to raise money for war bonds after pressure from the Pittsburgh Courier, which continued to advocate for Dorie Miller. They pushed for him to go as well, like white war heroes did. A week after the Pearl Harbor attack, Dorie Miller was assigned to the USS Indianapolis. He spoke in Oakland, California, his hometown in Waco, and he had the opportunity to address a graduating class of African-American sailors.

Unfortunately, Dorie Miller did not survive the war. In the spring of 1943, Dorie was called back to service and was assigned to a different kind of ship called an escort carrier. This was the **USS Liscombe Bay**. A Japanese submarine fired a single torpedo into the ship hitting it in the worst possible location, causing the bombs on the ship to explode. This resulted in the loss of 644 men and only 272 survivors. The ship sank in just 23 minutes. It was one of the deadliest attacks on an American ship during the war. Dorie along with his fellow shipmates, had no chance to make it to safety. At first Dorie was listed as missing, but a year later he was officially presumed dead.

Doris "Dorie" Miller did not live to see the United States and the world triumph over Nazi Germany and the Japanese Empire. He did not live to see an integrated military as ordered by President Harry S. Truman in 1948, nor did he live to see segregated signs removed from public spaces. Beyond a doubt, what Dorie Miller did on December 7th, 1941 would lead to changes on how African-Americans were viewed and their capabilities in the military. His actions on that Sunday morning demonstrated beyond a doubt that a person can rise to the occasion of heroism, regardless of their color.

In 2010 he was featured on a U.S. postage stamp. Who knows how many doors Dorie opened for the generations of young men of color who came after him?

(Source: US Postal Service)

As we learned earlier, Dorie Miller received the Navy Cross for his actions, but it is never too late for Congress to act and award him the Congressional Medal of Honor for his heroism and courage. There have been efforts to award Dorie for what he should have received when he was alive. Congresswoman Eddie Bernice Johnson of Texas has been an important voice in this endeavor, but you can act and make your voice heard as well! If Dorie Miller's story inspired you, contact your senator and representative and urge them to support Dorie Miller being awarded the highest honor that Congress can bestow upon a citizen. Your voice matters. Let's keep his story alive!

Timeline of Dorie Miller's life and Remembrances

1919- *Dorie Miller is born in Waco, Texas*

1939- *Enlists in the United States Navy*

1940- *January- Transferred to the USS West Virginia. Served on the USS Nevada at Secondary Battery School. Returns to the USS West Virginia*

1941- *December 7th, USS West Virginia was attacked. Dorie Miller fights back heroically*

1942- *Dorie Miller is awarded the Navy Cross by Admiral Chester Nimitz*

1943- *Reassigned to the USS Liscombe Bay and is promoted to the rank of Mess Petty Officer, Ship's Cook Third Class*

Dorie Miller along with over 600 other sailors die on the Liscombe Bay was torpedoed by a Japanese submarine.

1970- *Portrayed by Elven Havard in the movie Tora! Tora! Tora!*

1973- *The United States Navy commissioned a frigate, the USS Dorie Miller in his honor*

1991- *Commemorative plaque dedicated in his honor by the Alpha Kappa Alpha Sorority at the Miller Family Park at Pearl Harbor*

2001- *Portrayed by actor Cuba Gooding Jr. in the movie Pearl Harbor*

2010- *The U.S. Postal service issues a stamp with Dorie Miller's image*

2017- *On the 76th anniversary of Pearl Harbor, a 9-foot bronze statue of Dorie Miller was unveiled in Waco, Texas.*

Glossary of Key terms and People

Admiral Chester W. Nimitz (1885-1966)- Commander of the U.S. Pacific fleet in World War II. Held command over land, air and sea forces in that region.

A Phillip Randolph (1889-1979)- African-American labor and Civil Rights leader in the 20th century. Organized and led the Brotherhood of Sleeping Car Porters. He was one of the key leaders and organizers of the March on Washington in 1963.

Double V- This was a two-part victory campaign that African-Americans waged in World War II: Victory over racism at home and our enemies overseas.

Fair Employment Practices Committee- Established by President Franklin D. Roosevelt's executive order banning discrimination in the war industries.

Frank Knox (1874-1944)- Secretary of the Navy under President Roosevelt for most of World War II

NAACP- The National Association for the Advancement of Colored People. Established in 1909, this is the nation's largest and oldest Civil Rights organization

Navy Cross- This is the Navy's second highest award for valor in combat. This was what Dorie Miller was awarded. Those who served with him during the Japanese attack felt that he deserved more.

Pearl Harbor- Served as the Naval base of the United States Pacific fleet before and during World War II. On December 7th, 1941, the base was attacked by the Japanese, plunging the United States into World War II.

Plessy vs. Ferguson- Supreme Court decision in 1896 that mandated 'separate but equal' facilities which legalized segregation for the next 68 years in the United States.

President Franklin D. Roosevelt (1882-1945)- Longest serving President of the United States. He was first elected in 1932 and re-elected in 1936, 1940, and 1944, and served as President during the Great Depression and World War II. Prior to his presidency, he was Secretary of the Navy and Governor of New York.

Segregation- The practice of separating people by race

Sharecroppers- People who worked on land owned by someone else who received a share of the crop for their services. This was life style of many African-Americans in the South after the Civil War and into the 20th century.

Tuskegee Airmen- A decorated group of African-American fliers in World War II. Also known as the "Redtails", they had an exceptional combat record battling the Airforce of Nazi Germany.

USS Liscombe Bay- Escort carrier commissioned by the Navy during World War II. Was sunk in 1943 with a tremendous loss of life.

About the author

Dante R. Brizill has been a Social Studies educator for the last 15 years in Delaware and Maryland. He earned a Bachelor's degree in History from Hampton University and a Masters in Teaching degree from Wesley College. A native of Philadelphia, he is a die-hard fan of the Philadelphia Eagles. His hobbies include reading, writing, and traveling. He resides in Delaware with his wife and children. A lifelong history buff, Brizill has always been passionate about helping young people recognize the contributions of all Americans. Stay tuned for his next book!

Interact with the author! Follow on Instagram *@historyteacher81* **and like the Facebook page** *Dorie Miller: American Hero* **for updates and announcements about this book and events.**

Now That You've Finished the Book

…..Let's have a discussion!

Share your answers with someone who has read the book, your classmates or book club.

1. What is something about Dorie Miller's life that is similar to yours, or someone you know?

2. Why do you think Dorie Miller was seeking to join the military at the time he did?

3. How do you think Dorie Miller felt about only being trained to load the ships guns and not fire them, or only being responsible for cooking meals and serving?

4. Why do you think African-Americans supported the war effort despite unfair treatment and being forced into lesser roles?

5. Why do you think the US Navy at the time only allowed African-Americans to be messman?

6. What in Dorie Miller's childhood do you think prepared him for his actions on December 7th, 1941?

7. How important was the newspaper the Pittsburgh Courier was in making sure Dorie Miller was recognized for his actions?

Extend Your Learning

1. Pretend you are a reporter that had the opportunity to interview Dorie Miller after the attack. Come up with five questions you would ask, and the answers Dorie Miller would have given based on what you learned.

2. Why were battleships named after states? When did that practice begin? Research why and share your answers.

3. Give the date when African-Americans were finally officially allowed to be more than mess attendants and cooks in the United States Navy and explain how this came about.

4. After researching the standards for the Congressional Medal of Honor, compose a letter to your local Congressperson explaining why you think Dorie Miller should be awarded this honor for his actions on December 7th, 1941.

Bibliography

Books

1. Cutrer, Thomas W and Parrish T *Doris Miller, Pearl Harbor, and The Birth of The Civil Rights Movement,* Texas A&M University Press, 2018

2. James, Rawn, Jr. *The Double V: How Wars, Protest and Harry Truman Desegregated America's Military.* New York: Bloomsbury Press, 2013

Web sources:

1. www.blackpast.org
2. www.navalaviationmuseum.org
3. www.nationalgeographic.com
4. www.awesomestories.com

5. https://americacomesalive.com/2012/02/20/dorie-miller-1919-1943-hero-of-world-war-ii/

Articles:

1. Patrick S. Washburn (1986) The Pittsburgh *Courier's* Double V Campaign in 1942, American Journalism, 3:2, 73-86, DOI: 10.1080/08821127.1986.10731062

Made in the USA
Columbia, SC
28 July 2019